VIKING

OUTSOURCING

HELP WANTED

Web developer,

Graphics artist,

Blog writer,

Virtual assistan

Viking Outsourcing Page

Chapter 1:

Intro to Outsourcing

Whether you're starting a business or launching a new project within a well-established company, hiring a freelancer may be a new experience for you. Freelancers are a great way to bring specialist expertise to your group, especially if that expertise is not needed long-term. Freelancers are often flexible and cost-effective, but it can be difficult to know how to find the right match for your project. This book will help you to outsource effectively and find a freelancer that will provide you with high-quality work.

This book will guide you through the process of finding a freelancer that suits your project and will help you to build your business. As the freelance industry grows and more industries incorporate freelancers into their teams, now is the time to learn about this valuable asset.

Freelancers are self-employed workers who are hired by clients to provide specific services, usually on a short-term contract basis. The most popular areas for using freelance workers are as follows:

-     Software and web development

-     Writing; particularly copywriting and technical writing

-     Teaching and tutoring

-     Graphic design

-     Sales and marketing

-     Virtual assistance and administration

Of course, these are just some positions on the ever-growing list of skills you can find through freelancers. Every year, more people are joining the freelance workforce, and the idea of employment is evolving. "Hiring the best person for the job" can now be applied to individual projects rather than long-term jobs, meaning that you can hire writers or developers who have specific experience with similar projects. This allows employers to save time and money that would otherwise be spent on training a long-term employee every time a new type of project began. Freelancers are often hired online and work remotely, which also saves employers the cost of renting office space. Freelancers are a great way to keep costs down while still receiving top-quality work.

If you're considering hiring a freelancer but unsure about whether or not it's the right choice for you, consider the pros and cons below.

Pros:

- You'll save money by not paying for employee benefits, tax, pension, or office space, supplies and maintenance.
- Freelancers are easy to replace if they aren't a right fit.
- Freelancers offer high quality work at all times, whereas a full-time worker may have highs and lows. Freelancers are aware that they need to impress every time in order to secure more work in the future.
- Access to the best person for the job, regardless of location.
- Only hire them when you need them; you aren't paying people all the time regardless of the amount of work.

- Very specific and diverse work experience that people who have been doing the same job for years probably don't have. This experience may also have made them aware of new ideas and practices that can benefit you.

Cons:

- They may not be available immediately or to the full extent that you'd hoped, as they might have multiple contracts.
- They don't have as much knowledge of the company and your workflow as a long-term employee.
- Not as committed/loyal to the company as a long-term employee; they may choose another client over you if they are offered better terms.

- Working with someone far away can create awkward communication through time differences and slow down the project.

Outsourcing is ideal if you are a small company, if you need a position filled for a short amount of time, or if you need a person with specific skills and experience. Many freelancers also like to commit to recurring work with their clients, so you can build a professional relationship with a freelancer and teach them more about your company over time.

Chapter 2:
Where to Find Them

You have a job and you want a freelancer to fill it- how do you connect the two? Right now, the most popular way to hire freelancers is through online platforms. These platforms allow you to post jobs that freelancers can see and apply for; you can also browse freelancers' profiles and contact any that you think might be a good fit for the position.

There are some platforms that only cater to one kind of freelancer: for example, Zirtual provides virtual assistants and sites like 99 Designs, DesignHill, and DesignContest provide graphic designers. Below are breakdowns of five of the biggest and most popular freelance platforms.

Many of these platforms use escrow, meaning that the client's money is saved by the site when your contract begins and released to you when the work is completed. This can provide great security when working with unknown clients.

Upwork

Upwork is one of the most popular freelance platforms around and has over 1.5 million users, including every job type that freelancers are used for. Freelancers are verified by Upwork administration and are reviewed by the client after every completed job, so you can read their reviews before hiring them. When you post a job on Upwork, you can post how much you are willing to pay, the expected amount of time the job will take, and the level of experience you would like the freelancer you employ to have.

The money you pay is put into escrow when the contract begins and is released to the freelancer once you confirm the work is complete. This ensures that both the client and freelancer are financially protected.

PeoplePerHour

PeoplePerHour is mostly aimed at web projects, but all positions can be advertised. This means there are more marketing and software developer freelancers on this site, but you will also be able to fill a writing or graphic design position. Freelancers must pay to use

PeoplePerHour once they have sent 15 proposals to clients, which means there are a smaller number of users.

Guru

Guru is a company that has grown hugely in the past decade, with more than 1 million jobs completed. Guru's freelancers can upload a portfolio of their work for potential clients to examine before hiring them. Freelancers can see how much a client has spent through the site before working with them to see if they are viable and how much they can expect to earn. Guru is similar to Upwork in its inclusion of portfolios and client reviews.

Toptal

Toptal does not cater to all freelance areas; it exclusively provides web developers, designers, and finance experts. Toptal is also exclusive when it comes to the freelancers themselves; the site employs an extensive screening process and only accepts those with a high level of experience. It boasts that it only accepts 3% of the freelancers that apply to the site. This high level of member expertise means that rates on Toptal are higher than other sites.

Freelancer

Freelancer allows freelancers to browse and apply for jobs according to their skill level. As well as hourly and long-term contracts similar to other sites, Freelancer offers "contests", where a client posts a job with a money prize, and freelancers bid on the project with their submissions. This style means that freelancers must put in more work for jobs that they may not get, but allows potential employers to see exactly what they'll be paying for.

When you have decided which site(s) to use, take some time to browse other jobs before posting your own. What job details are clients mentioning upfront? Are they offering hourly or flat rates? It can also be useful to browse freelancers' profiles to see what you can expect from the people who apply for your position. Freelance profiles will also give you a good idea of how much is considered a reasonable rate of pay. If you aren't sure exactly how long a project will take, at least give an estimate. Freelancers will be organising other jobs to begin after working with you, so it's unfair to expect them to act as if they only work for you.

Chapter 3:

Working with Them

Hiring a freelancer isn't the same as hiring an in-house employee, so working with a freelancer won't be the same either. When you begin to work with a freelancer, it helps to establish a few things as soon as possible.

Rate of pay

Freelance contracts are usually either paid at an hourly rate or a flat fee. You may have stated how much you are offering for the job in your proposal, or you are willing to negotiate. A freelancer may want to discuss exactly how much work is involved in the project in order to determine their fee. If you decide to pay by the hour, most freelance platforms have time management devices that allow you to monitor exactly how much time the freelancer has spent working. If you decide to pay a flat fee, many freelancing platforms allow you to split that fee into sections based on milestones within the project. All of these details should be negotiated with the freelancer before the project begins.

Method of communication

Many freelance platforms have rules that prohibit freelancers from communicating with clients outside their sites. This is because these sites keep a portion of the freelancer's fee; if the freelancer is paid outside of the site, the platform doesn't make a profit. Each freelancer will tell you if communicating outside the platform you met through is a problem for them. If you use the same freelancer more than once, you may choose to not communicate via a freelance platform after the first job. Email and Skype are also popular ways in which clients communicate with freelancers. Your company probably has an established form of communication, such as Slack. It may be easier for you to ask the freelancer to join such a site, but it may be an unnecessary step if you aren't working together for long.

Establish workflow

It's important to remember that this will be different to workflow with an in-house team; time differences and physical separation will make working with a freelancer a different experience. Keep this in mind when you first work with freelancers and allow yourself to figure out what does and doesn't work for you. Once you've established a new kind of workflow, working with freelancers will be just as easy as working with in-house employees.

The key to any workflow is organization. Figure out what you'll need from the freelancer before you post the job on a platform, and communicate those needs at the beginning of the contract. This will make things easier for everyone involved. Remember that the freelancer doesn't know as much about the project as you or an in-house employee would, so you may need to provide them with more information than usual.

Conclusion

When outsourcing work to a freelancer, it's important to work sequentially. First, you need to decide if a freelancer is the best choice for your project. Freelancers are best suited to short-term projects, new companies and groups that wish to save money that would otherwise be spent on a full-time employee.

If a freelancer is right for you, you'll need a network in which to post your open position. The sites listed in Chapter One each have their benefits, so look at those that sound best for your project and sign up for one. Browsing these platforms will give you great insight into the freelance marketplace, both in terms of what you can expect from freelancers and what they will expect from you.

When you start a contract with a freelancer, you will need to adapt your workflow for this new style of teamwork but once you do, you'll reap the unique rewards that come with outsourcing. Low costs, high quality and on-demand specialists will all be part of your next project!

www.ingramcontent.com/pod-product-compliance
Lightning Source LLC
Chambersburg PA
CBHW040931210326
41597CB00030B/5265